A Biography:
My Life
As a
Basset Hound

By Katie the Blue Heeler

As Told By: Ellen B. Collins

PublishAmerica
Baltimore

First printing

ISBN: 1-4137-8776-2
PUBLISHED BY PUBLISHAMERICA, LLLP
www.publishamerica.com
Baltimore

Printed in the United States of America

Dedication:

To my mom, for making me smile and showing me what life was all about. Wait for me, okay? I have tons of kisses for you! –Katie

Table of Contents

Introduction

This is a true story about Katie, my blue heeler, who was raised with my two basset hounds, Marty and Suze. Katie's story begins with her trip from Elgin, Texas, to Round Rock, Texas, where most of the mischief, mayhem, and loving occurred. Katie will tell you how she learned to do many things during her lifetime; for instance, walk like a basset hound, how she learned to smile, how she learned to let me know when she wasn't feeling well, how she learned compassion for her basset hound brother and sister, how she knew the definition of the word "love," and how she carried it through her whole life. She'll tell you just how happy she was at times, how sad, how wet and dirty, how she learned to say "I love you," how funny, how smart, and what stupid things she did as a puppy and as a grown-up (and should have known better). We (Marty, Suze, and I) hope you enjoy this story about our Katie. She taught all of us a lot about life, love, and happiness. And mostly, she taught us how to smile!

Chapter One:

My Humble Beginnings

My life as a basset hound began in the fall of 1997. One day, while playing with my siblings in my pen, these two people—a man and a woman—came by and chose me to be their new baby. I surely didn't want to leave my brothers and sisters. Why, what would they do without me!! My brothers and sisters were the only family I knew and grew to love. We played all day and learned a lot of stuff from our mom. Who would they have to chase and pick at their heels and herd together at night? I was sure these people made a mistake in choosing me. Nevertheless, I saw the happy look on the lady's face, and I thought, *okay, let's try this.*

Little did I know that this was just the beginning of my journey as a basset hound. I was going to find out that I had another brother and sister waiting for me at home. Their names were Marty and Suze. And you guessed it, they were basset hounds! I had never seen anything like them before. Low to the ground, they kept stepping on their ears, which was just the funniest thing I ever saw. Every time they stepped on their ears, their heads would go sideways! How could someone have such long ears and keep stepping on them all the time? I found out later that their ears were great to bite and keep the basset hounds in line. If I really wanted to have some fun with them, I would step on their ears and watch their chins hit the floor! So, every time I wanted a laugh, I would step on their ears and watch their chins hit the ground! I found out also that just because you are low to the ground and short, it doesn't mean that you cannot run fast! It was just amazing to me! When Marty and I would play tag in the backyard, his ears would be in the air flowing on either side of his head!! He looked so funny and his face—I thought he was smiling, no really! Smiling!! I think he enjoyed playing with me in the backyard. He couldn't run for long, because his legs were short and had some kind of bone problem, so did Suze. After a few minutes, they had to rest...and rest...and sleep...and rest...until it was dinnertime! Then, after eating, it was outside, more potty training, and running for five minutes! Then it was time to come in, get some lovin' from the lady we called "mom," get up on the couch with Mom, and watch silly TV shows. Basically we just get rubbed and kissed. Suze learned early the best spot in the whole house was on top of Mom's chest, so she crawled up there after dinner and fell asleep. I stayed on the floor so I could protect them. Then Marty would sit at the end of the couch with his shoulders up on the arm rest of the couch. He looked like a little human sitting there, with long ears!

So, my life as a basset hound began. I was trained by both Marty and Suze to keep my head low to the ground and sniff. If there was a smell I didn't know or Marty and Suze didn't know, we marked the scent with our feet! Yep, with our feet. We would make sure that the oils from the bottom of our feet were right on top of or near that new scent, just in case we happen to be walking the backyard again and needed a good whiff! Now, I also learned this: when you find a really good smell in the backyard, you drop to the ground over the smell and roll on top of it with your legs in the air. My goodness, the first time I saw this I thought both Marty and Suze were sick or having problems. They later explained it to me that a good scent was one to rub your body over, and then shake all the excess grass and leaves off of you, but the scent remained. It also gave the place where the scent was our body smell too! And it told anybody who might want to get into our backyard, that this was *our yard* and to *back off*!!

Now, I didn't totally take over being a basset hound; I still enjoyed being a blue heeler. You see, I am the kind of dog that is used for herding cattle and sheep. Our natural tendencies are to nip at the heels of any stray sheep or cattle and get them back into the group, so that everyone is safe and we can all go home for dinner. Well, my herding was limited to getting Marty and Suze up and into the house when Mom called. Yeah, we called her Mom and even learned how to say "Mom." We even learned how to say "I love you, Mom." We practiced that in the backyard and in our pens when Mom was at work and we got bored. I know she loved us; she told us all the time. She would sleep on the floor with us, let us get on the couch (even though we weren't supposed to!), and give us extra treats like liver and sometimes oatmeal cookies! She was the best! When she took us all for a walk, I started my basset hound training by sniffing and getting to know my neighborhood, just like Marty and Suze. Sometimes, I would stay back a little just to make sure that I watched them and how they were sniffing some things. Now, of course, there were always going to be some things that Marty and Suze didn't want to sniff, and they told me so right away. They would keep me from sniffing something bad, like another dead animal, a dead bird, or even some remains from another dog. There was a park across the street where we lived and there was a drainage ditch. When it rained, the ditch filled up with garbage and lots of water and it was awful, just awful. Marty and Suze would bark and bark and bark until I walked away from the area; they didn't want me to sniff the bad stuff and get sick.

So, I learned over the months to do quite a few different things. I learned that in the morning, it was time to go outside and walk the backyard for any signs of new scents or see if there was any other evidence that someone else had been in our backyard. One morning, it was really interesting. It had just finished raining and Mom let us out in the backyard. We all saw something moving really fast in the grass. We had never seen anything like it. It was dark and long and moved really fast. So Marty told me to go and "get it." So I put my foot on it and grabbed it with my mouth and held it down. Marty then told me to take it to Mom and show her. When I brought it into the house to show Mom, she wasn't very happy, but she was worried. You see, what we found was a snake in the grass of the backyard. Mom was concerned that it might be a poisonous snake and somehow might hurt us. So, very quickly, she checked me over. I seemed fine, and she put the snake in a plastic bag. She ran upstairs to the room where she spent a lot of time, it had a computer...yeah, that's what she called it. She looked it up on the computer, and it was nothing but a harmless garter snake. She asked me to show her where the other snakes were. So, I did, and I got Marty and Suze to go with me to make sure we didn't get into any trouble! Mom got rid of the other snakes and said it was okay again for us to play in the backyard. We didn't see any more snakes for a long, long time there.

And then the next thing I learned was how to move like a basset hound. Okay, so I didn't have long ears like they did, or short, stubby legs like they did, but hey, I was willing to give it a try. I kind of got down on my knees and tried to move like Marty and Suze. I just couldn't do it, my legs were too long. So I compromised and just stood straight up and moved slower, a *lot* slower than I'm used to doing. Hee hee, it was fun! I was funny to look at too, because I put my neck between my front legs and wobbled along! I think secretly Marty and Suze were laughing at me, but I have to admit, it must have been funny to look at!

So, here I am, only a few months old and finding out that my fears of going to a new home were just vanished and gone because I found a most loving and caring home with a nice lady who loves me very much. She gave me baths, and she cleaned my face. She talked to me all the time and gave me kisses on my face. I scrunched up my face when she did, because it's not just one kiss, there are *tons* of kisses every time! You get used to them. After she gave them to me, I smiled back at her. Yep! I learned to smile. Living with two basset hounds you gotta learn to laugh. They are funny-looking to begin with, *then* on top of that, they just keep doing funny things, like stepping on their ears and breaking a *lot* of wind. I mean a *lot* of wind. Marty is really good at doing that and when he does, he looks at everybody else to see if they notice anything different. He also burps and when he does, his jowls move. I'll show you pictures of Marty and Suze later, and you can see what I mean.

Anyway, let me get on to more of how I became an unofficial basset hound. First of all, we live in a state called Texas. Now, in Texas, it doesn't do what the northern states do during winter; it doesn't snow here. At the most it gets very cold and the wind blows really hard, but it never snows here. A couple times a year it rains a lot. Mom is always there to wipe us down. Afterwards, yep, you guessed it, a *ton of kisses*!! She must have tons to give and she gives out a lot!!

Chapter Two:

Marty 'n' Me

It seems we are getting older. We are about a year old now (seven years in doggie years), and we are still considered youngsters and do get into trouble every now and then.

Okay, so let's recap on what I've learned in my first year as the unofficial basset hound. I have learned to walk slow and deliberate, so I can smell everything around me, even when the June bugs hide in the ground. I can smell them under the dirt. It's fun to dig them up though. They don't like it when we try to bite them, and they fly away really fast, only to dive bomb back into the ground again! More fun for us! Hee!

Now, to see Marty and Suze try to bat *anything* with their short legs is just a hoot in itself. Sometimes, when I'm lying on the grass in the backyard, I can see Marty out of the corner of my eye and he is trying desperately to keep a twig in his mouth by trying to hold it down with his paws!! *Not gonna happen!* He just cannot do it, but he just doesn't realize that he cannot do it. The more he tries, the funnier it gets! Until he hears me laughing, he is concentrating very hard on what he is trying to do. When he does hear me laughing, he stops immediately and walks over to me as if to say, "Hey, you think you could do better?" So, I shake my head "yes" and go over to the stick, bring it over to him, sit down, and put it between my two front legs and hold it down that way and show him I can reach it. Then I show him something he didn't know how to do. I'll put the stick in my mouth, flip over onto my back, and while on my back, take my front paws and hold the stick. I can reach it better that way. "Hrmphhh," says Marty, and he asks for the stick back. So, I give it to him smiling, and he goes off a little way across the backyard. When he stops, he looks around to make sure nobody is looking, and then he throws himself onto his back on the ground with the stick in his mouth, his paws up in the air and sure enough, he can reach it with his short, stubby paws!! He is so excited that he drops the stick, gets up, and runs around the backyard, stopping short only long enough to bark at me and tell me what I already know! Gees, he's a funny guy indeed! And so, here we go again with Marty teaching me and I'm teaching him; it's a wonderful relationship with this brother of mine. Sometimes, I just sit in the backyard and stare at him and Suze. They are so different than me and none of us look the same, but Mom loves us all so much! How could one lady love us all so very much? I hope to spend my whole life finding out.

This is a really funny story that I am about to tell you. Mom had this really long and large couch; it seemed to go on forever. One day when Marty, Suze, and I were out of our cages and Mom was away for a little while. You see, when we started to get older, she trusted us outside of our cages for about an hour or two each day and left the house to see if we would either behave ourselves or get into trouble. Well, we mostly got into trouble when she left us out.

This couch Mom had was the ugliest thing in the house, and when you rubbed up against it, you couldn't help smelling something different every time. Well, I thought that I wanted to take a taste of what I smelled that morning and so I just took a little nip at the couch. All of a sudden, a piece of the couch was in my mouth. *Oh my goodness*, I thought, *Mom is going to kill me!* So, I turned around to Marty and Suze to ask them what I should do. They came over and without a word to me, after sniffing the area around the hole in the couch, started pulling on the couch. Within a few minutes or so, we had all the fabric off two cushions, and the foam cushions chewed up and all over the floor and ourselves! Man, we looked silly. We were having the best time, and we didn't even think of the consequences of getting in trouble, until we heard the back door. Mom was standing there with her mouth open, not believing what she was seeing at all! Here we are with foam and fabric all over our heads, our ears, our bodies, and trying to spit out any remains of foam, hoping she wouldn't think it was our fault. You should have seen the three of us. We had foam everywhere, and foam was still falling to the ground when Mom walked in and caught us all. Well, at first she looked mad, and then she started laughing, because we all looked like we were trying to be so normal, that it came across as funny. How could Mom be mad at us now? She brushed all the foam off of all three of us, very lovingly, and let us go outside for a while, while she cleaned up the place. I felt bad that Mom had to do all the cleaning, but she had a smile on her face when she did, saying something like, "I was hoping that couch was going to go sometime...now I guess it's time to get a new one!" We were always testing Mom in some way! Hey, it was our nature!

Chapter Three:

Suze "Alpha" Basset Hound 'n' Me

Now, let me get to Suze. She is a doll, no, really! She is what is commonly referred to in the dog world as an "alpha" dog. She is the one who gets all the grooming from Marty and then from me. I seem to be the low dog on the totem pole since I am the youngest, so I don't get groomed at all, except by Mom. She knows the pecking order, and she knows that when Marty grooms Suze, and then Marty gets groomed by me, then it's *my turn* to get groomed by Mom. She gets the brush out, brushes me, gives me a tummy rub, cleans my face off with a wet cloth, and then—you guessed it—*tons of kisses!* Oh my goodness, the first time Mom ever blew on my stomach, it was such a funny noise, I jumped up and looked at her with my head turned to one side, as if to say "what was that?" I eventually got used to Mom blowing on my tummy. After a while I began to smile. I trusted Mom so much; I let her touch my paws, my face, my tummy, my whole body. Sometimes Mom's touch was so comforting that I would fall asleep in her arms while she was giving me a rub. So my Mom knows that I'm last in the order of dogs here, and even after knowing all that, she loves me so very much, not any more or any less than the other two.

Now Suze and I got into some trouble when we were babies. For some reason or another, we enjoyed it when Mom was taking a shower. Both Suze and I would jump on the bath tub and try to catch the water as it was coming out of the shower head. The first time it happened, we got showered with the foam from the shampoo that Mom was using on her head. When Mom finished her shower and opened the curtain, there we were, both of us with foam all over our heads! She looked at us like how could that have happened! We looked funny, I know we did. From that day forward, Suze and I just loved being near Mom when she took a shower. We'd get covered. I think it was because we enjoyed our baths so much, that's why we liked being sprayed by the water.

Since Suze was the first girl dog in the house, she told me right away that it was *her house* and *her mom* and I'd better get used to being third dog around here. I told her that since I was new I didn't understand right away her passion and feelings for this lady she called Mom. I learned over the year that Mom was the one person you could trust, who took care of us, our needs, knew when we were sick, and knew when to make us smile again. It's amazing to me how Suze felt about Mom. It's a very strong feeling, Suze told me one day. It's a feeling that just overcomes you. One day you look at this lady who takes care of you with not that much feeling, and then the next day, you are just a sap for her and find that you cannot live without this lady's love and affection. The fact that she gives us great snacks, is another thing altogether!

Suze spent days telling me how wonderful Mom could be, how hard her life was with the man who was living there, and how she chose to hide her sadness by giving us all the love she could muster. It was a real tough story to hear, but Suze said this one thing to me. She overheard Mom one day telling the man in the house that by no means would she ever choose to give us up for anything! You see, the man didn't like us very much and stayed away from all of us, not just me. We didn't seem to care for him either. He never petted us and he *never* kissed us and hugged us like Mom did. We knew right away there was something wrong with the man. One day Suze said, "We'll all probably move out with Mom, because she needs to be happy and told the man that she can be happy with me and the basset hounds, since the man has already moved on and started a new life of his own."

Suze and I got to talk a lot about some of the things that went on in the house. I understood more about why Mom was so loving to us and put all her effort into us in making us feel like her children. It was because the man who lived with us didn't love her any more and so she turned all her affection and caring to us. Suze told me sometimes, when Mom wasn't looking, she would see Mom crying. Suze told me that she would come up to Mom and hug her as if to tell her it was going to be alright. Mom would give her a huge hug and the love that came out of Mom's eyes for Suze showed immensely. Sometimes, Mom would talk to us when she was feeling down. We knew it and would sometimes lift her arm up so we could get closer to her, as if we were telling her that things were okay. They were going to be okay, because me and the basset hounds, you see, we were a team and Mom was our team leader. We loved her very much. Then sometimes, Marty would do just the funniest thing and get everybody laughing again.

After we all moved, we moved into a much smaller place, but we had Mom all to ourselves. Mom had to work two jobs to make end's meet, but she always came home for lunch to let us outside and always came home for dinner to feed us. Most times, Mom wouldn't eat until she was done with her second job, but that was Mom. She made sure that we were taken care of. Both Suze and Marty were lifted up onto Mom's bed at night and I slept, once again, at the foot of the bed to make sure nobody would get us and Mom would be safe. We never had any problems with anyone.

Then, after another year, we moved into a huge house. It had a doggie door and a huge backyard that we could all play "tag" in, and we did. Man, I would get the basset hounds, especially Suze, all excited in a game of tag, and since Suze was so slow, I would tag her, run back into the house through the doggie door, get some more water and maybe a snack, and sit by the patio door to watch Suze try to find me. I know it wasn't nice, but it was so funny, the look on her face, when she realized I wasn't there. What she would do when she turned around and saw that I had been staring at her the whole time through the patio door! She would lie down and just giggle until she couldn't stand it. Then I would go back outside through the doggie door and lay down next to her. Yep, I would put my paw on top of hers, and she knew that she had found a true sister in me.

There were so many times when Suze could be the true alpha dog, and then there were times, when we would just sit on the patio, not having to say a word to each other, just understanding that we enjoyed each other's company. Of course, I knew full well that Suze was the boss of all of us and that was the best sister a dog could ever have. One thing about basset hounds, they are loyal. Not only are they loyal to their owners, but they are loyal to their siblings in that they try so hard to keep you from getting hurt or in trouble. That doesn't mean that they don't like getting into trouble themselves, it just means that they are very protective and watch you all the time. You see, because of their keen sense of smell, they know when there is danger around. They will bark to let others know they are there, then they will stand very close to you to protect you from that danger until they know that everyone is safe.

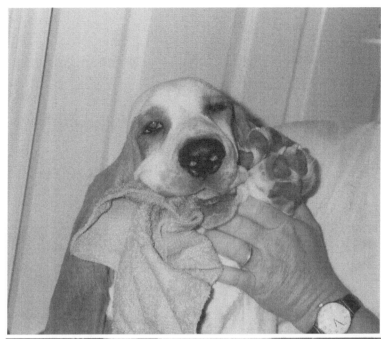

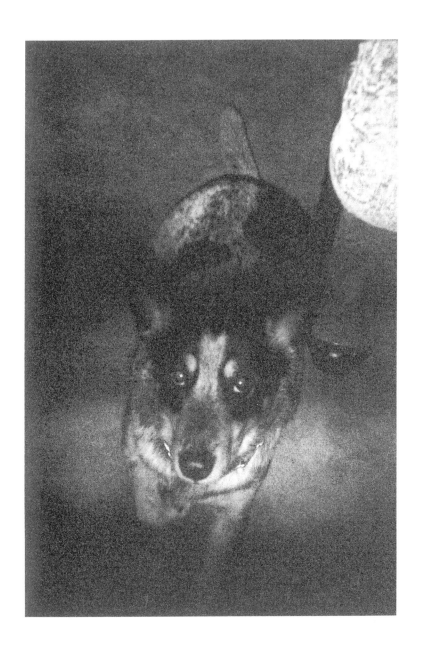

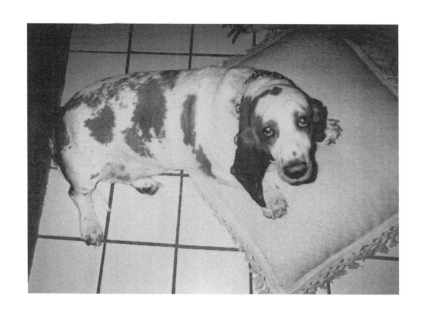

Chapter Four:

The Ever Playful and Growing Years
As an Official Basset Hound

Another thing was getting used to the move. We always knew when Mom was moving again. She would bring home all these boxes and things would get put away and shoved into places and packed up. The very last thing to go would, of course, be the three of us. Every time Mom took a box out to the truck, we wanted to go with her. Sometimes we nagged at her feet until we slipped out the door with her. She had to run to catch us, but we didn't get far. Marty would start whining, and within an hour or so, he would have Suze so riled up. I would have to stand by Suze and tell her that everything was going to be okay. You just couldn't calm Marty down. He would run around the house or apartment and collect all of his toys, make sure there wasn't any food in the bowls, and sit on top of his blankets with his toys and whine. We just didn't want her to forget us. We knew in our hearts that she would never forget us. She always tried to make a better living for us, no matter where we were. It showed in the places we moved to and the things we saw. Especially on our walks; man, we loved our walks. There were new places and new smells and new sights to see. There were also new dogs in the neighborhood to get to know when were walking. We all would talk for hours to each other. It was great fun.

It was great fun learning to pick our noses. Yep, that's what I said. Mom thought it was a disgusting thing, but it really was a necessary thing. You see, every once in a while, we would get something stuck up our noses. Whether it was a leaf, a piece of food, or more foam (hee!). Naturally, the only way to get it out was to literally pick our noses. We would put our paws on our face and start at the top of our noses and work our paws all the way down to the end of the nose, hoping that whatever it was that was stuck, would work its way out. When that didn't work, we would sneeze. Most of the time, we would get in front of Mom and sneeze all over her. Sure enough, she would just scrunch up her nose and have the worst look on her face. "Disgusting," she would say. She would always get up, warm a washcloth under the sink, and wash off our faces, hoping to get the last remnants of whatever we sneezed out.

I was continually learning that basset hounds don't just have big ears, they have long tongues too. On the rare occasion that I was groomed, Marty would come by and sit down in front of my face and begin to clean me. He would start out by my ears and work his way all over my face. Needless to say, his tongue was huge! He could take one lick and get the entire side of my face. I didn't complain, because it felt good. It felt good to get groomed, other than having Mom do it, since I know she had so much stuff to do most of the time.

We all learned to scratch each other's backs, since we all needed each other every once in a while. By that I mean that whenever one of us got into trouble, the others would step up and help with the blame so nobody was singled out. That's called "sibling love." We had plenty of it. Usually, it was Marty who got into trouble. When he did, I would get right next to him to make sure Mom didn't spank him. He was the only one that got spanked, probably because Mom just thought he did all the bad stuff himself. Really, when Mom would just get onto him, both Suze and I would rally around him and make sure that we let her know it just wasn't his fault. If you wanted to spank one, you had to spank us all. Suze and I would just bark until Mom gave up and sat down. So, we scratched each other's backs a lot and it was worth it, because the love we all felt for each other. We knew Mom was trying to teach us right from wrong, but we had to make sure that we were all so very close ourselves. Suze was the only one who rarely got yelled at. I think it was because of her eyes. She has really long eyelashes and a real girly look to her. Mom always cradles her face and just looks into her eyes. Suze has a way of working Mom so that Mom just looks at her and she melts.

Yep, sometimes we would poop outside of our cages (only when we were sick, though). That's how Marty and Suze got their nicknames, Poopey Toes and Starfoot. Suze would inevitably step in something, and Mom started calling her Poopey Toes. Whenever Marty used to stretch or try to relax, his feet would spread out and look like stars, so Mom called him Starfoot. Also, when Marty would step in something, it would leave the impression of a star on the tile floor or concrete, so I learned to be the proud sibling of Poopey Toes and Starfoot.

When we were all young, Mom put us in crates while she was at work. It was to train us not to go potty in our sleeping area, and then at night when she came home, we would have access to water and dinner!! When Marty and Suze were babies, they had some kind of digestive "bug" that kept them in the doctor's office a lot. I worried sometimes that I would never see them, they were gone so much. I understand that that is what basset hounds have. They have bad digestive systems when they are young. Mom was always giving them some medication. This particular medication would give them diarrhea. Since we were training not to poop in our pens, Marty and Suze would raise their tails up, turn around so their butts were facing the back of the cage, and poop outside of the cage! Yep! Poor Mom! When she got home there was just a mess for her to handle. She never got mad, though. She always let us out of our pens, made sure that Marty and Suze were okay, and let us spend some time outside. It always took them a while to get used to their medicine when they hadn't taken it for a while. So that's the pooping outside the cage incident. It stopped after they were about a year old, since their stomachs didn't get sick any more and Mom basically had us outside our cages now for most of the day. We also conned her into sleeping with us at night. Hee, actually it was the other way around that she would let us sleep with her, but we all enjoyed being on the bed together, snuggled up.

When we were babies, Mom would lie down on the bed and put each of us, at different times of the afternoon, on top of her chest and stomach, so we could be close to her heartbeat. Sometimes when we were little, we would fall asleep listening to Mom's heartbeat, hoping we'd always hear that beautiful sound that made Mom who she really was. Suze really liked lying on Mom's chest. I remember for about the first year or so, she would climb up on Mom's chest and take her afternoon nap up there. Mom never said a word; she would always just stroke us and make sure that each of us would get our naps up there. Mom was never too busy for us; she made time in her day. Sometimes all afternoon, when we weren't feeling well, she would take the time to let us sleep, get our rest, or just be with us.

Well, let me tell you that going to the doctor was an event at our house. None of us, even when we were little, wanted to go to the doctor at all. We remembered when we were very little that the doctor gave us shots, messed with our ears, clipped our toenails, and made our tails stand straight up in the air! So none of us wanted to go to the doctor unless all of us went at the same time. That way, we all could watch out for each other and could tell the stories later when Mom had to run out and get groceries or run errands.

We were the best nurses that a dog snack could buy! Mom had a lot of surgeries on various parts of her body. We were always worrying about Mom when she had surgery, making sure that nobody got to her, so she could get better and rest. Marty especially got into anybody's face that came near her. That was his mom and no one was going to hurt her. We would wait until Mom was situated on the bed, but of course, she had to lift Marty and Suze up there. It was hard when she had her hand surgeries, but she wanted us with her, so she got them up there; it took a while, but she accomplished it. We would all pick a spot and lie down next to her and protect her so she could not move around much. That was our job, protect and love Mom at all times.

Oh my goodness! Let me tell you about our first heavenly interlude with Starbucks. Mom went one Sunday morning to Starbucks to get her Venti Mocha Frappucino (I think that's what she called it) oh yeah, with extra whip cream on top! Anyway, she would always get a snack for us when she was there. We would each get a bagel for Sunday morning. Then, Mom would ask us all to sit down and we would get a taste of whip cream, not the chocolate, because it was bad for us, but we would get a taste of that whip cream. I think I smiled every time I had the opportunity to taste that. What an amazing taste. Mom wouldn't give it to us all the time, but on Sundays, that was a special day. We were allowed to savor the flavor of the Starbucks bagel and whip cream breakfast.

The only other day that was even more special than Starbucks Sundays, was Christmas Day. Mom would buy us presents and wrap them. However, she couldn't put them under the tree because we would sniff them, tear them open, and eat them before Christmas. So on Christmas Day, and we knew when it was Christmas Day, we would get Mom up early. She would make a cup of coffee and disappear into her bedroom only to come out a short time later with three packages. She would make us sit and then give us our brightly wrapped package. All of us would wait until we had a package and then we'd rip into them. Sometimes it would be pig ears, or a toy, or a velvet bone, but it was always something good. Later on, when Mom was taking a shower, we would laugh and jump for joy, knowing that our Christmas Day was again a very special time. The only thing we ever had to give Mom was our thanks. We would just roll her over sometimes with how excited we would get in thanking her! She would be covered with dog kisses and barking and watching each of us run around the apartment. It was a great day indeed. We always got to share some of Mom's special Christmas Day dinner. She almost always had turkey and would share that and a little bit of gravy with us. Life was grand indeed!

At one time or another, we all found out that silk flowers and stems do not taste very good, but they sure do leave sparkle on your face and nose. My mom had a room where she did all of these floral arrangements and plant baskets. She would go to craft shows and sell them (or not). On the Sundays that she would need to make more of them, she would open up the door and let us in. Marty would lay down by Mom's feet (usually) and Suze and I would stay farther back. Marty, you see, was Mom's baby boy and had a couple more privileges than we did. It didn't bother us, because we knew we were just as special to Mom in her heart. Anyway, sometimes I would stick my nose in a bag of those flower supplies that Mom had because they smelled good. Well, I would find something in her bag that sparkled and looked good, so I would sniff it and rub against it. By the time Mom noticed me, I usually had silver sparkles all over my face and nose and was caught with the flower stem in my mouth! I know Mom wished she would have had a camera sometimes, because there were times when I would just look plain ol' goofy and nothing could be done about it! Sometimes, I would pick a flower stem that was old or just made of something nasty and couldn't get the taste out of my mouth. I would leave the room and kept sneezing, wondering when the smell would go away. Sometimes, Mom would poke her head out of the room to see if I was okay, and I would be on the blankets in the hallway with my paws over my nose, just wishing I would have listened to her when she told me no in the first place. I stayed away from flower stems after that!

Chapter Five:
Mom 'n' Me

I guess you never really know what to expect from life until you live it to your fullest. That's what I did when I met my mom so many years ago. You see, I had no idea that she would be this nice, loving, caring, fun lady who basically would be spending the next six years with me, Marty and Suze, raising us, loving us, disciplining us (which, according to Mom, didn't happen all that much!), and just being with each other. I never realized how wonderful a person she was. Sometimes, when I was feeling down, I'd jump up on the couch and put my left front paw on her leg and just looked at her for reassurance that everything was going to be okay. And, you know, it was! Mom rubbed my paw, put her arms around me, and all was better! She made me feel so wanted and so loved—gees—there just isn't any way to express those feelings that I felt for her, other than to say I hope you experience it for yourself.

To watch Mom all those years, knowing when we were going to have a snack and get to play individually with Mom (which was so much fun, because it was different for all of us). You see, there were things I could do that Marty and Suze couldn't do. They had to sit on the back porch while Mom threw the ball into the backyard and we would play catch for quite a while. I think Marty and Suze got tired just from watching us play. Then when Mom would sit down to rest a while, Marty and Suze would join us on the porch and we'd all do a group hug. It was neat to see everybody close their eyes just at that right moment when Mom gave us this big squeeze. Then, of course, there were her *tons* of kisses! She never stopped kissing us, even when she was mad at us; she never stopped kissing us and loved us all very much.

Getting to know Mom all those years and watching everybody in our house grow and get older, was a wonderful thing. I guess I was one of the lucky ones who found a loving family to go to. I wish I would have kept up with my siblings over the years to see if they went to as good a home as I did. There just wasn't any way for me to stay in touch with them. Not having a thumb kind of hindered us from writing anything and how would we do it? How could our paws communicate? We just had to leave our lives up to those people who took us in, hoping that we are treated well and loved. I will always feel bad for those dogs whose family just doesn't love them. Sometimes, when Mom took us for a walk, we'd see other dogs that were just slapped and smacked around. They would tell me as they passed me that they wanted so much to come with me and the basset hounds. Every time they saw us walking, Mom would be petting us, or giving us water if it was hot, or just making our walk special, like when the marathon runners came by, we would grab a concrete log and sit down, and Mom would wave to them as they went by. Other dogs noticed that and told us about how lucky we were, as if we all didn't know that!

Sometimes, in the evening, when Mom was laying on her bed all alone, I would sneak up there and get close to her and lay on a pillow. All Mom had to do was tell me to come closer. When I did, I just lay down on her chest and enjoyed her company. She would talk to me, tell me about her day, and tell me how she loved me, all while rubbing my face and my chest and back. After about an hour, she asked me to go get Marty and Suze and let them know it was time for bed. So, I did. When Mom gave me the signal, I would round them up and get them to come into the bedroom from the living room. I told them Mom was sleepy and it was time to go to bed, so I could protect everyone. Just like clockwork, those basset hounds knew what I was saying. As they followed in a line behind each other, Mom would lift them up onto the bed. She would wait until they found their positions, and then she'd lie down on the part of the bed that was left. Mom always gave us the most comfortable part of the bed. Sometimes, Mom would wake up with an awful back ache or neck ache, but she would never move us over. She wanted us to be comfortable, and she loved us very much.

Conclusion:

The Sunset of My Life

You know, every day was a blessing for me to have been loved so much by one human being and to constantly have the love of a brother and a sister (even though they still look a little funny to me at times!) I am now five years old, and we all moved from the house in Round Rock to a really small apartment in South Austin. It was a place that just the four of us could be together in. We all shared the bed—that's right, all of us—with Marty and Suze snoring and farting in the middle of the night. I would start out on the bed, but my job was to make sure no one came near us, so my spot was on the floor in the middle of the room. That way, with my keen sense of hearing and clearly out of range from Marty's snoring, I could hear if anybody was either coming in the front or back doors or trying to get into our room, then alert Mom that something was wrong. Yep, I did a great job for my mom; after all, it was all I could do for her giving me such a special life, right?

There were times, I know, it wasn't easy for Mom. She

worked two jobs to make sure the bills were paid and we had dog treats, got our walks in the morning, at noon and at night, got our baths, and spent the rest of the time just plain loving all of us with all of her heart and soul. Yep, so protecting my mom and Marty and Suze was a full-time job. You see, when Mom went to work in the morning, she would always rub my head and tell me to make sure I took care of my brother and sister. I told her I would never let her down with one great big bark!

After we passed our teenage years, Mom would allow us to be out of our cages and just sleep on the tiled portion of her apartment. In the summer it was really cool, and Mom always took care of us. She gave us tons of blankets and pillows, because you see, Marty and Suze still had bad bones and needed the extra padding so they didn't hurt so much. They also got some medicine every night to make sure it didn't get bad! When it was possible, Mom would get a bag of pig ears and we'd be so happy!!! We would thank her afterwards by licking her hands, and she would rub our faces and tell us how much we meant to her. Man, I couldn't have asked for a better life.

I didn't have any problems with my bones or my heart or anything that would cause Mom to worry. I was the healthy one, or so I thought. One morning, I got up with Mom and she took us for our morning walk, gave us a treat, and got ready for work. Before she left, she did her usual and patted us all on the head and told me to make sure everybody was protected today. I tried to smile at her but couldn't. She noticed and asked me what was wrong. I just sat down, I couldn't tell her anything. I know this worried Mom, and she gave me a hug (and it hurt a little, I was surprised at that!)

and told me she would be home for lunch to check and make sure I was okay. She then left for the day.

I started out my day as usual: went to the water bowl, got a drink, and then was walking down the front hall to get to the blankets and thought, *I just don't feel good and if I just make it to my blankets, I'll be fine. I just need some rest.* I couldn't make it to my blankets and told Marty and Suze that I wasn't feeling well. As a brother and a sister, they gathered around me—each of them sat on either side of me—and put their heads on me, as if to tell me it was going to be okay, that all I needed was some rest. As I was laying down, I felt really strange, like I couldn't breathe and when I tried to tell Marty and Suze, I just didn't have enough breath in me to let them know and let out a great big sigh and felt very, very tired. As I put my head down, I remembered everything about my life. I remembered the day Mom came to get me, the day I got eight baths all in a row because I had fleas on me, the first time I saw Marty and Suze, the first time I had some ice cream (and wasn't supposed to!), the first time I learned how to walk, talk, act, sleep, and live like a basset hound. Most of all, I remembered learning how to smile at my mom for giving me such a wonderful life. That last thought that very last thought was in my mind before I went to sleep. And I went into a deep, deep sleep to a world I never saw before.

When I woke up, I could see my mom. She had come home from work for lunch and noticed the two basset hounds still by my side, not moving and I wasn't moving either. She felt me and I was cold. There I was, up above her, trying to let her know that I was okay, that I could breathe alright, that my chest didn't hurt. I was jumping up and down, telling her this, but she couldn't hear me. I remember her calling work and telling them that Katie passed away, and I didn't understand what she meant. When I saw her hit the floor on her knees and cover her face, I knew something was wrong.

Sometime that morning, I passed from my life to a different world, a world where everybody there was somebody's babydoll or just like me, had been raised a basset hound, even though we weren't. It was an eternal playground where we could look down on those who loved us, and right now, the one who loved me was crying uncontrollably. She stopped for a minute, Marty and Suze still by my side, went into her bedroom, brought out a blanket and very, very lovingly wrapped me in the blanket. Marty and Suze immediately became upset because Mom was taking me somewhere and they weren't sure what happened to me; they just knew I wasn't my usual self.

Mom took me to the vet's office where they told her that apparently I just died in my sleep. I didn't have any health problems, but I guess it was time for me to go. It is so painful watching from above how my mom was handling all of this. She was crying and gave me one last hug. Then she brushed my face with her hands. As she did when I was alive, she kissed my face all over, as if to reassure herself that I knew she was there and I was still her babydoll.

The rest of the afternoon was a blur for Mom. She didn't go back to work, and when she came back to the apartment, Marty and Suze were still in the same spot where I laid down and died. It was two weeks before Marty and Suze would move from that spot, often barking and pawing at it, as if to bring me back, but all the while knowing I wasn't coming back. I know my brother and sister were sad and expressed it when Mom wasn't around. They would talk to each other about me and remember all the fun times we had. Why, they even talked about what a pain in the butt I was (sometimes, not all the time!). Yeah, we all loved each other very much, but I can say that I cannot wait until I am reunited with Marty and Suze again and Mom, too. I'll find them! I'll find them all! Until then, I'll be watching over them to make sure nothing ever happens to them.

So, there you have it, my life as a basset hound. It was a great life, and I hope you enjoyed my story. I know Mom has put some photos in here of me, Marty and Suze and maybe one or two of herself, so you can see what everybody looked like. My favorite picture of me is when Mom took us to a doggy daycare, and they took our pictures there. I am smiling so big because we had fun the whole day, playing and sniffing and getting to meet other dogs. It was a good day and when they took my picture I was really smiling big!

Epilogue

I had such a great life with Mom and Marty and Suze. We all learned a lot about life, about loving, about sharing, learning to definitely get along with each other, and most of all, learning to smile! Always take care of yourselves and always be good to each other, have fun when you can, laugh and love all the time. Looking back on all those years, I never would have changed a thing. I'm waiting for you, Mom, with *tons* of kisses!

Love, Katie.

Oh, and don't forget to look at all the neat photos of us and of Mom!